Creating a Dispensary (legally)

Creating a Dispensary (legally)

Matthew Petchinsky

Creating A Dispensary (Legally)
by Matthew Petchinsky

Disclaimer

This publication is intended strictly for informational and educational purposes only. It is not legal advice, financial advice, medical advice, tax advice, or business guidance specific to your situation. The content contained herein represents the author's research, opinions, and experience at the time of writing and is provided as general information to help readers understand key concepts regarding dispensary establishment and operations in regions where such businesses are permitted by law.

While every effort has been made to provide accurate, current, and lawful information, the laws governing cannabis, hemp, and CBD-related businesses — including cultivation, retail, manufacturing, distribution, and marketing — vary significantly by country, state, county, and municipality. These laws are evolving rapidly and are subject to change without notice. Therefore, the information in this book may not reflect the most recent legal or regulatory developments in your specific jurisdiction.

The author, Matthew Petchinsky, and Apophis Enterprises LLC make no warranties or guarantees, expressed or implied, about the accuracy, completeness, reliability, legality, suitability, or applicability of any content presented in this book. The examples, references, and scenarios are for illustrative purposes only and should not be interpreted as endorsements, guarantees, or definitive business advice.

You are solely responsible for ensuring that any action you take, including but not limited to establishing a dispensary, selling hemp-derived products, or marketing CBD-related items, complies with all local, state, and federal laws and regulations. You are strongly encouraged to consult with appropriate licensed professionals, including but not limited to:

- Attorneys specializing in cannabis or hemp law
- Certified public accountants (CPAs) familiar with cannabis industry taxation
- Licensed business consultants with hemp/CBD experience
- State regulatory agencies or health departments

Nothing in this book should be interpreted as promoting or endorsing the illegal use, sale, possession, or distribution of controlled substances. This book does not advocate for the use of products that are prohibited in your jurisdiction. It also does not offer or imply medical claims, therapeutic advice, or guarantees regarding health outcomes. All products discussed are intended for legal adult use where permitted and should be used responsibly.

Readers should also be aware that certain terms (e.g., "dispensary," "CBD," "Delta-8") may carry legal definitions that vary by jurisdiction and may have implications for business registration, product categorization, and law enforcement interpretation.

Use of this book does not establish any kind of professional-client relationship between the reader and the author, publisher, or any affiliated entity. The author and publisher expressly disclaim all liability for any loss, harm, injury, legal consequence, or financial damage resulting directly or indirectly from the use or misuse of the information contained in this book.

By reading this book, you acknowledge and agree that:

1. You are solely responsible for your actions.
2. You will independently verify all facts and laws before implementing any advice.
3. You release the author and publisher from any liability or legal claims.

Introduction: The Green Gold Rush Begins

We are living in a once-in-a-century shift — a moment in history where what was once criminalized and hidden in the shadows is now becoming one of the most promising, profitable, and socially accepted industries in the world. And at the center of that transformation lies the modern hemp and cannabis dispensary.

Not long ago, the idea of opening a legal store to sell cannabis-derived products would have been unthinkable for most people. Today, dispensaries are appearing in suburban strip malls, downtown storefronts, online shops, farmers' markets, and wellness expos. Hemp-infused oils, legal THC gummies, CBD beverages, and topical creams are now stocked on retail shelves in everyday stores — not just in fringe backrooms or underground collectives.

And here's the truth: this opportunity is still **early**. The world is still catching up.

This book isn't about pipe dreams. It's not some stoner fantasy. This is a grounded, strategic, and legally sound guide to **building a real dispensary business** — online or physical — with products that are 100% compliant under current federal U.S. law (and in many other countries as well). It's your blueprint to launch smart, build fast, stay safe, and grow into a legitimate legacy brand that serves real people while creating real wealth.

Whether you're brand new to the industry or have a background in wellness, e-commerce, retail, or entrepreneurship, this book will give you the edge you need to step confidently into a rapidly growing field that combines personal freedom, community healing, and cutting-edge commerce.

Why This Book Exists

The biggest challenge most aspiring dispensary owners face isn't money. It isn't branding. It isn't even competition.

It's **uncertainty**.

They're unsure if it's legal.

They're unsure how much it costs.

They're unsure what products are allowed.

They're unsure how to market without getting banned.

And they're unsure if it's possible to succeed without millions in funding.

This uncertainty paralyzes would-be entrepreneurs — and allows the industry to be dominated by large corporations with deep pockets, legal teams, and lobbyists.

This book was written to eliminate that uncertainty.

Inside, you'll find clear, direct answers to the most pressing questions, including:

- **Is it legal in my state to start a hemp dispensary?**
- **What licenses do I need?**
- **How do I avoid breaking the law?**
- **Can I do this online without a storefront?**
- **How much will it really cost to get started?**
- **What products are safe, legal, and profitable to sell?**
- **How do I advertise without getting shut down?**
- **How do I protect myself from financial or legal risk?**
- **Can I grow this into a lasting, full-time business?**

The answer to all of these is: **yes** — if you follow the right steps.

Who This Book Is For

- Aspiring entrepreneurs who want to enter the cannabis space legally and ethically
- Wellness advocates looking to create trusted hemp-based product lines
- Retail store owners wanting to add compliant cannabis-derived products to their shelves
- E-commerce professionals ready to sell hemp and CBD products online
- Side hustlers seeking a low-cost business with recurring customers
- Dreamers who are ready to turn their vision into a grounded, legal brand

You do **not** need to be a lawyer. You do **not** need a cannabis license (in many cases). You do **not** need a giant warehouse or seed-to-sale system. You need a **plan, knowledge**, and the **willingness to follow the law better than your competition.**

What You'll Learn

Each chapter of this book is designed to walk you through a key part of the dispensary-building journey:

- **Chapter 1:** What is a dispensary? Defining the legal difference between hemp and marijuana
- **Chapter 2:** Is it legal in your state? Understanding the 2018 Farm Bill and your local regulations
- **Chapter 3:** Online vs. physical dispensaries — which path is right for you?
- **Chapter 4:** Registering your business legally — LLCs, EINs, licenses, and protections
- **Chapter 5:** Sourcing legal, high-quality, compliant hemp-based products
- **Chapter 6:** Marketing in a restricted industry without getting banned
- **Chapter 7:** Financing your dream and launching on any budget
- **Chapter 8:** Scaling your brand and building lasting customer trust

The appendices also include **recommended tools, a sample startup budget**, and a **launch checklist** to make implementation fast and simple.

The Rules Are Changing — Are You Ready?

We are in a post-prohibition moment for hemp. The stigma is cracking. Laws are evolving. Consumer demand is soaring. And yet, very few people understand how to build a legal dispensary without getting burned.

If you wait for "perfect" clarity, you'll miss the wave. But if you step in with preparation, compliance, and strategy — you could secure your space before the rest of the world realizes what's happening.

This is the **green gold rush** — and you don't need millions or an MBA to join it. You just need the right roadmap.

This Is Not a Promise — It's a Playbook

This book won't guarantee you success. That's your job. But it **will** give you the most current, comprehensive, and accessible strategies available for entering the hemp dispensary world legally and confidently.

You're not just selling products. You're building a brand. You're shaping perception. You're participating in one of the most important economic shifts of the 21st century — one rooted in wellness, entrepreneurship, and reclaiming sovereignty from outdated systems.

If you're ready, the green path is open.

Let's begin.

Chapter 1: What Is a Dispensary?

Before diving into the legal complexities, startup costs, and marketing strategies, we must start with a fundamental yet often misunderstood question: **What is a dispensary?**

In popular culture, the word "dispensary" is often associated with marijuana — the kind that gets you high. But in the real world of modern, legal commerce, a dispensary can take many forms, and its meaning is entirely dependent on legal definitions, THC thresholds, and your specific jurisdiction.

In this chapter, we'll clarify what a dispensary really is in today's marketplace, the difference between marijuana and hemp, the two core categories of dispensaries, and why understanding this distinction is vital to building a compliant, successful, and profitable business.

Defining the Modern Dispensary

A **dispensary** is any licensed or legally registered retail or online business that sells cannabis-derived or cannabis-related products. These can include oils, topicals, gummies, flower, beverages, and other wellness items made from either marijuana or hemp.

However, not all dispensaries are created equal — and not all are legal everywhere.

There are two primary types of dispensaries:

1. Marijuana Dispensaries

- Sell products containing **more than 0.3% THC** (tetrahydrocannabinol), the psychoactive compound that causes a "high."
- Only legal in states and countries where **recreational or medical marijuana** has been legalized.
- Require **extensive state licensing**, product tracking systems, security measures, and often millions in startup capital.
- Operate under **heavily regulated environments** that can change rapidly.

2. Hemp/CBD Dispensaries

- Sell products derived from **industrial hemp**, containing **less than 0.3% THC by dry weight**.
- Federally legal in the United States under the **2018 Farm Bill**.
- Can be operated **online or in-person** with significantly fewer regulatory hurdles.
- Products include **CBD oils, Delta-8 (where permitted), topicals, hemp flower, and THC-free edibles**.
- Startup costs can be as low as **$400 to $800**.

This book focuses **exclusively** on the second category — **legal hemp-based dispensaries**. These businesses are not only lawful in many parts of the United States (and internationally), but also represent one of the **most accessible paths to building generational wealth** in a green economy.

Hemp vs. Marijuana: The Legal Line That Matters

To understand what you can and cannot sell in your dispensary, you must grasp the legal distinction between **hemp** and **marijuana**.

They are both part of the **Cannabis sativa** plant family, but they are treated entirely differently under U.S. federal law.

Plant Type	THC Content	Legal Status (Federal)
Marijuana	More than 0.3% THC	Federally illegal (Schedule I)
Hemp	0.3% THC or less	Federally legal under the 2018 Farm Bill

This **THC threshold of 0.3%** is the dividing line. Hemp is considered a non-psychoactive product, while marijuana is considered a controlled substance. If your product **exceeds 0.3% THC**, you are potentially violating federal law — and subject to criminal penalties.

What Can You Legally Sell in a Hemp Dispensary?

A well-run hemp dispensary can offer a wide variety of consumer products, provided they remain within legal boundaries and have proper lab documentation (COAs — Certificates of Analysis). Here are examples of **compliant, in-demand products**:

- **CBD Oils and Tinctures**: Used for anxiety, sleep, and general wellness. Non-intoxicating.
- **Gummies and Edibles**: THC-free or compliant levels of Delta-8/Delta-10 where permitted.
- **Topical Creams and Balms**: Applied to the skin for pain relief or inflammation.
- **Hemp Flower**: Looks and smells like marijuana but contains less than 0.3% THC.
- **CBD Vapes**: Available in some states; highly regulated.
- **Functional Beverages**: CBD-infused teas, coffees, and sparkling waters.

◈ **Important:** Not all states allow every category of hemp product. For example, smokable hemp is banned in some areas, and Delta-8 THC is under increasing scrutiny. Always check your local regulations.

Why Clarity is Your Competitive Advantage
Most people are confused about cannabis laws. The internet is flooded with misinformation, outdated advice, and fear-mongering. That confusion creates hesitation — which leads to inaction.

Your advantage as a business owner is clarity.
When you fully understand what you're legally allowed to do — and what you're not — you gain confidence. And confidence turns into action. Action turns into a real, thriving business.

Customers are also looking for trusted sellers. When you can articulate the legality of your products, show them lab results, and offer honest information — **they will come to you instead of the shady store down the street.**

Myth-Busting: Common Dispensary Misconceptions

Let's address a few common myths:

- **Myth 1: "You need a license to open any dispensary."**
  ◇ Not true. Hemp-only dispensaries often do **not** require special cannabis licenses — just standard business registrations and compliance with your state laws.
- **Myth 2: "Selling CBD is illegal."**
  ◇ CBD derived from hemp (with less than 0.3% THC) is federally legal. However, product types may be restricted by state or city.
- **Myth 3: "Dispensaries require massive investment."**
  ◇ You can start a compliant online hemp store for **under $1,000**, often even less.
- **Myth 4: "If it's sold online, it must be legal."**
  ◇ Not necessarily. Many online sellers are out of compliance or breaking state-specific laws. This puts their businesses — and customers — at risk.

Why This Matters More Than Ever

We are standing in the early stages of a green economic revolution. The demand for hemp-based wellness products is surging. Public perception is shifting. Federal laws are evolving. And small entrepreneurs, not just corporations, are carving out lasting wealth.

But this industry still carries **stigma**, **scrutiny**, and **regulatory risk**. Those who rush in blindly can lose everything. But those who enter **strategically, legally, and clearly** — with quality products and transparent practices — will be the ones who **own the next decade**.

Key Takeaways from Chapter 1

- A **dispensary** can be legal and compliant if focused on **hemp-derived** products (not high-THC marijuana).
- The **0.3% THC limit** is the key legal line between hemp and marijuana.
- There are two dispensary models: **marijuana (high-cost, high-barrier)** and **hemp/CBD (low-cost, accessible)**.
- Hemp-derived products can be sold **online or in-person**, provided they follow federal and state rules.
- **Clarity and legality are your competitive advantage** — not a barrier.

Chapter 2: Is It Legal in Your State?

One of the most important — and confusing — questions any prospective dispensary owner must ask is:

"Can I legally sell hemp-derived products where I live?"

Unfortunately, a simple yes or no isn't enough. The legality of opening a dispensary, even one focused strictly on hemp and CBD products, depends on a complex combination of **federal**, **state**, and sometimes even **local laws**. To operate safely and confidently, you must understand where these legal lines are drawn, how they interact, and how to stay in compliance.

In this chapter, we'll break down:

- The role of the 2018 Farm Bill
- The difference between federal legality and state-specific rules
- How to find out what's legal in your state
- Common legal pitfalls to avoid
- How to stay compliant while selling online or in person

Let's clear the fog and give you the legal clarity that most people never get.

The Federal Foundation: The 2018 Farm Bill

In December 2018, the **Agricultural Improvement Act of 2018** — commonly referred to as the **2018 Farm Bill** — fundamentally changed the landscape of hemp in the United States. This single piece of legislation is what opened the door for millions of legal hemp-based products and the rise of CBD and Delta-8 THC sales.

Here's what the Farm Bill did:

◈ 1. Removed hemp from the Controlled Substances Act

This meant that hemp — previously considered the same as marijuana under federal law — was **no longer a Schedule I drug** if it contained no more than **0.3% THC by dry weight**.

◈ 2. Legalized hemp cultivation, processing, transport, and sale

As long as the THC content remains below the 0.3% threshold, hemp is now federally legal to grow, ship, and sell — even across state lines.

◈ 3. Shifted oversight from the DEA to the USDA

Instead of being treated like a dangerous narcotic, hemp is now considered an agricultural commodity, regulated by the **U.S. Department of Agriculture (USDA)**.

◈ 4. Allowed for the sale of hemp-derived cannabinoids

This includes **CBD, CBG, CBN**, and other non-psychoactive compounds — and, in some interpretations, **Delta-8 THC** and similar cannabinoids derived from hemp (though these are increasingly controversial at the state level).

In summary: if your product is **derived from hemp** and contains **less than 0.3% THC**, it is legal at the federal level.

But that's only half the picture.

The State-by-State Puzzle

Even though hemp is federally legal, individual **states have the authority to impose additional restrictions**. This means a product that's legal under federal law may still be restricted, limited, or outright banned within your state or county.

Every state falls into one of four categories when it comes to hemp retail laws:

Category	Description	Examples
◈ Fully Legal	Most or all hemp products are permitted for retail and online sale	Colorado, Oregon, Florida
◈ Partially Restricted	Specific products (like Delta-8 or smokable hemp) may be banned	Texas, Michigan
◈ Heavily Restricted	Retail sales limited or allowed only through licensed programs	Utah, Iowa
◈ Illegal or Unclear	Hemp-derived products not allowed, or laws unclear and risky	Idaho, South Dakota (as of recent data)

How to Find Out What's Legal in Your State

Legal landscapes change frequently — sometimes overnight. That's why it's crucial to check **official state sources** before launching your dispensary.

Here's how to do it step by step:

◈ Step 1: Search for Your State's Hemp Laws

Use this phrase in a search engine:

"[Your State] hemp laws 2025 site:.gov"

This will return official government websites, rather than unreliable blog posts or forum chatter.

Check your state's:

- Department of Agriculture
- Department of Health
- Department of Licensing
- Cannabis Control Commission (if applicable)

◈ Step 2: Identify Key Legal Areas

Look specifically for:

- **Retail restrictions** (Can you sell to the public?)
- **Product limits** (Are smokables or Delta-8 allowed?)
- **Labeling requirements** (Do you need to include lab results or disclaimers?)
- **Licensing or registration** (Do you need a permit, or can you sell freely?)

◈ Step 3: Consider Local Laws

Even if your state is hemp-friendly, **your city or county may have its own zoning rules** or storefront bans. Always contact your **city clerk** or local business licensing office to ask:

- Are hemp/CBD retailers allowed in this area?
- Are there restrictions on signage or product types?
- Do I need a local business license in addition to a state one?

Online Sales: Are They Legal?

Yes — with conditions.

Most states allow **online sale of hemp-derived products** as long as:

- You only ship to states where those products are legal
- Your products contain **under 0.3% THC**
- Each product has a valid **Certificate of Analysis (COA)**
- You don't make unproven medical claims

If your product meets those conditions, you can **run a fully legal online dispensary** that ships nationwide — with a few exceptions.

◈ States to Watch Carefully (Subject to Change)

Some states are especially strict or unclear when it comes to hemp-derived cannabinoids like Delta-8 THC:

- **Idaho:** Only allows CBD with 0% THC (even trace amounts are illegal)
- **South Dakota:** Vague or unfriendly toward certain cannabinoids
- **New York:** Bans Delta-8 and other synthetically derived cannabinoids
- **Alaska, Colorado, Vermont:** Specific bans on certain products despite overall legalization

Always verify before shipping or promoting products across state lines.

What If I Want a Physical Store?

If you plan to open a **brick-and-mortar dispensary**, you'll likely need:

- A retail business license from your state and/or county
- A hemp retailer registration (if required by your state)
- Compliance with **zoning laws** (not near schools, for example)
- Security plans, signage restrictions, and health inspections in some areas

This is where consulting a **local attorney or compliance specialist** can save you tens of thousands in fines and months of wasted time.

Common Legal Pitfalls (And How to Avoid Them)

1. **Selling products with >0.3% THC**
   Even a slightly over-the-limit result makes your product federally illegal. Always confirm **lab reports** from trusted suppliers.
2. **Shipping to banned states**
   Even if a customer orders, it's your job to **cancel and block the shipment** if it violates their local law.
3. **Making unverified medical claims**
   Statements like "cures anxiety," "treats cancer," or "replaces pain meds" are illegal under FDA rules. Use terms like "supports relaxation" or "promotes wellness" instead.
4. **Ignoring labeling requirements**
   Your products may be required to list dosage, cannabinoid content, batch number, and a link or QR code to the COA. Stay updated with your state's laws.
5. **Assuming hemp = automatic legality**
   Always verify with government sources — not influencers or hearsay.

Legal ≠ Easy — But It's 100% Doable

Operating a legal dispensary means **understanding the rules better than your competitors**. That's your secret weapon. Clarity is what gives you the edge in this space.

If you can:

- Source compliant products
- Avoid restricted states
- Register your business properly
- Avoid risky claims
- Stay up to date with state rules

...then you are ready to launch with **confidence and integrity**.

Key Takeaways from Chapter 2

- The **2018 Farm Bill legalized hemp federally**, but states still control how it's sold locally.
- You must check both **state** and **local laws** before launching your dispensary.
- **Online sales are legal** in most cases if you avoid restricted products and states.
- Avoid making **medical claims**, and ensure all products have a valid **COA**.
- Legal compliance builds your **reputation**, **trust**, and **protection** from enforcement.

Chapter 3: Online vs. Physical Dispensaries — Which Path Is Right for You?

Now that you understand the legal foundation of dispensaries and the federal-state landscape, the next big decision is this:

Do you want to launch an online dispensary, a physical store, or both?

This choice will shape your startup costs, daily operations, marketing strategies, legal requirements, and even your long-term growth potential.

Each path comes with unique benefits and drawbacks — and depending on your goals, resources, and location, one may be significantly better suited to your situation than the other.

This chapter will walk you through a detailed comparison of both models, outline what's required to get started, and help you choose the dispensary model that aligns with your vision, lifestyle, and budget.

The Two Dispensary Models

Model Type	Description
Online Dispensary	A legally compliant e-commerce store selling hemp-derived products to customers across your state or nationwide. Requires a website, product sourcing, marketing skills, and regulatory awareness.
Physical Dispensary	A brick-and-mortar retail location where customers visit in person. Requires a lease or building, licenses, signage compliance, retail staff, and zoning clearance.

Let's explore both options in-depth.

Option 1: Online Dispensary
◈ **Best for:**

- First-time entrepreneurs
- People with limited startup capital
- Home-based business owners
- Digital marketers, influencers, or content creators
- Those who prefer flexibility and mobility

◈ Advantages of Online Dispensaries

1. Low Startup Cost

You can legally launch an online hemp-based dispensary for as little as **$400–$800**, depending on your chosen platform and product inventory. No rent, utilities, or storefront buildout required.

2. Nationwide (and Global) Reach

A well-marketed online store can reach customers across the country — and even internationally where laws permit — instantly scaling beyond your neighborhood.

3. Minimal Staffing

You don't need employees to start. Many entrepreneurs run successful dispensaries as solopreneurs using drop-shipping models or pre-built affiliate storefronts.

4. Lower Risk Profile

Operating online keeps you away from high-visibility legal risks that physical dispensaries sometimes face, like zoning disputes or storefront raids.

5. Greater Flexibility

You can work from home, travel, or manage your store part-time while keeping a day job or managing other responsibilities.

◈ Challenges of Online Dispensaries

1. Digital Marketing Restrictions

You won't be able to run paid ads on Facebook, Instagram, or Google. Organic growth and strategic content will be essential.

2. Building Trust

With no in-person interaction, you'll need to showcase **lab results (COAs)**, use clear branding, and collect strong reviews to build consumer confidence.

3. Shipping Compliance

You must be aware of restricted states and product bans (e.g., Delta-8 in certain states) to avoid illegal shipments.

4. Platform Limitations

Some e-commerce platforms (like Shopify Payments or PayPal) may restrict hemp sales. You'll need to choose hemp-friendly processors and checkout tools.

◈ What You'll Need to Start an Online Dispensary

- A business name and LLC
- An EIN (Employer Identification Number)
- A hemp-friendly e-commerce platform (like BigCommerce, WordPress + WooCommerce, or custom systems)
- A payment processor that accepts CBD/hemp sales
- Product sourcing from compliant suppliers with lab-tested COAs
- Website hosting and domain name
- Branded packaging (optional, but helpful)
- Email marketing tools (e.g., MailerLite, Beehiiv)
- Legal disclaimers and terms of use on your site

◈ Typical Startup Cost (Online)

Item	Estimated Cost
Domain Name + Hosting	$20–$100/year
Website Setup	$100–$500
Product Inventory	$50–$300 (or use affiliate/drop-ship)
LLC & Legal Setup	$49–$300 (plus state fees)
Email Marketing Tool	Free–$49/month
Total Estimated Range	**$400 – $800**

Option 2: Physical Dispensary
◈ **Best for:**

- Experienced entrepreneurs or investors
- Those with access to capital ($150K–$2M)
- Business owners in states with favorable retail cannabis laws
- Retail-focused entrepreneurs with strong local networks

◈ Advantages of Physical Dispensaries

1. Stronger Local Branding

Customers can see, touch, and talk to you in person. This builds trust faster and can lead to a loyal customer base.

2. Walk-In Foot Traffic

If you're in the right area (near wellness centers, gyms, or universities), foot traffic can drive steady daily revenue without constant digital marketing.

3. Increased Sales Per Transaction

In-store customers often buy more per visit. You can upsell, bundle, and educate on-site.

4. Easier to Build Community

You can host events, loyalty programs, tastings, and educational workshops — all of which foster community engagement and repeat business.

◈ Challenges of Physical Dispensaries

1. High Startup Costs
Opening a legal physical dispensary can cost anywhere from **$150,000 to over $2 million**, depending on location, licensing, renovations, and staffing.

2. Complex Licensing
You may need multiple licenses (retail, sales tax, hemp retailer registration, zoning clearance), each with application fees and renewal requirements.

3. Zoning and Location Constraints
Not every city or neighborhood allows hemp or cannabis retail stores. You'll need to find a compliant location and get approval from local authorities.

4. Higher Legal Visibility
Being a physical business means greater exposure to regulators, competitors, and community scrutiny.

⬦ **What You'll Need to Start a Physical Dispensary**

- All requirements from online dispensaries **plus:**
- A compliant retail location
- Commercial lease or property purchase
- Build-out and security installation
- Inventory for in-store displays
- State and local retail permits
- POS (point of sale) system and cash handling procedures
- Trained staff
- Legal advisors or consultants

⬦ **Typical Startup Cost (Physical)**

Item	Estimated Cost
Licensing Fees	$5,000–$50,000
Real Estate Lease or Purchase	Varies by market
Interior Build-Out & Security	$50,000–$150,000
Inventory	$20,000–$100,000+
Staffing (1st Year)	$60,000–$120,000
Legal & Consultant Fees	$10,000+
Total Estimated Range	**$150,000 – $2,000,000+**

◈ Online vs. Physical: Side-by-Side Comparison

Feature	Online Dispensary	Physical Dispensary
Startup Cost	Low ($400–$800)	High ($150K–$2M)
Legal Complexity	Moderate	High
Location Needed	None	Required
Staff Required	Optional	Yes
Customer Reach	Nationwide	Local only
Scaling Potential	Very high	Moderate
Speed to Launch	Fast (1–4 weeks)	Slow (3–12 months)
Ongoing Overhead	Low	High
Risk Exposure	Lower	Higher
Customer Experience	Digital only	In-person and immersive

◈ Which Path Is Right for You?

Here's how to choose based on your current situation:

- **Choose Online if you:**
    - ○ Want a low-cost, low-risk entry point
    - ○ Prefer working from home or traveling
    - ○ Have marketing or tech skills
    - ○ Need to start small and grow gradually
- **Choose Physical if you:**
    - ○ Have access to capital or investors
    - ○ Are located in a cannabis-friendly zone
    - ○ Have experience in retail or customer service
    - ○ Want a long-term, high-visibility local business
- **Do Both (Hybrid Model) if you:**
    - ○ Start online, learn the market, build your brand
    - ○ Then expand into a local store once you're profitable and confident

Key Takeaways from Chapter 3

- There's no "one-size-fits-all" answer — both models can be highly successful.
- Online dispensaries are faster, cheaper, and easier to launch for beginners.
- Physical dispensaries require more capital, licenses, and legal navigation but offer powerful branding and in-person engagement.
- You can always start small and expand over time — many of the most successful cannabis businesses did exactly that.

Chapter 4: Registering Your Business Legally — LLCs, EINs, Licenses, and Protections

Starting a dispensary isn't just about products, branding, or making sales. If you want to build a **real business** — one that earns legal income, protects your personal assets, and scales confidently — then it must be registered properly.

In this chapter, we will walk through how to:

- Choose the right business name and structure
- Form an LLC (Limited Liability Company)
- Get your EIN (Employer Identification Number)
- Open a business bank account
- Apply for any required licenses or permits
- Set up protections that shield you legally and financially

Registering your business isn't just a formality — it's your **foundation**. Without it, everything you build could collapse with one lawsuit, tax audit, or regulatory penalty.

Let's build your business the right way, from day one.

Step 1: Choose Your Business Name

Your business name is more than a creative decision — it must meet **legal**, **branding**, and **searchability** criteria.

⬦ **Guidelines for Naming Your Dispensary**

- **Be unique and brandable**
  Avoid generic names like "CBD Shop" or "Hemp House." You want a name that stands out and feels memorable.
- **Avoid restricted words**
  In some states, using the words "marijuana," "pharmacy," or "medicinal" in your name may require special licenses or be outright banned.
- **Check for domain and social availability**
  You want your brand name to match your **website domain** and **social handles**. This prevents confusion and makes marketing easier.
- **Follow your state's naming rules**
  If you form an LLC, the name typically must include "LLC" or "Limited Liability Company."

⬦ **Pro Tip: Run a name check on your state's business registry website to see if it's taken.**

Step 2: Form a Legal Business Structure (LLC)

What is an LLC?

An **LLC (Limited Liability Company)** is the most common and flexible business structure for dispensaries. It legally separates your **personal assets** from your **business operations**, so if something goes wrong, your personal finances are shielded.

◈ **Why Choose an LLC?**

- **Protects personal assets** (home, car, bank accounts)
- **Allows you to open a business bank account**
- **Makes your business look professional and trustworthy**
- **Offers flexible taxation options**

◈ **How to Form an LLC**

Option A: Do It Yourself

1. Visit your **state's Secretary of State website**
2. Search "Form an LLC" and follow the steps
3. File Articles of Organization
4. Pay the state filing fee ($40–$500, varies by state)
5. Designate a registered agent (can be you, in many states)

Option B: Use an Online Service

There are reputable services that can handle it for you, typically charging $49–$300 plus state fees. They often include:

- LLC filing
- Registered agent service
- Operating agreement template
- Annual compliance reminders

Either method is fine — the important part is that your LLC is **officially filed and approved by your state**.

Step 3: Get an EIN (Employer Identification Number)

An **EIN** is your business's equivalent of a Social Security Number. It's issued by the IRS and used to:

- Open a business bank account
- File taxes
- Hire employees or contractors
- Apply for business credit

◈ **How to Get an EIN**

- It's **free** from the IRS
- You can apply **online**, by fax, or mail
- You must already have an LLC formed (or be in the process)

Once approved, you'll get a confirmation letter with your EIN — save this in your business records. Most banks and service providers will ask for it.

Step 4: Open a Business Bank Account

Never mix your personal and business finances. Doing so opens you up to:

- Legal liability
- Tax complications
- Difficulty tracking business expenses
- Losing your LLC protections in court ("piercing the corporate veil")

◈ To Open a Business Bank Account, You'll Need:

- Your EIN letter
- LLC formation documents (Articles of Organization)
- A valid photo ID
- Business address (not a P.O. Box, unless it's a virtual mailbox with a street address)

◈ Choose a Bank That Supports CBD/Hemp Businesses

Some banks still discriminate against legal hemp-based businesses. Ask them upfront:

- "Do you support accounts for CBD/hemp retail?"
- "Are there any restrictions on product type?"

Also consider online business banks with less red tape and easier digital onboarding.

Step 5: Register for Licenses and Permits

This step varies **state by state**, but here's what to check for:
◈ **Common Dispensary-Related Licenses**

1. **Sales Tax Permit** (required in most states if you sell physical products)
2. **Hemp Retailer Registration** (required in some states for CBD sales)
3. **General Business License** (issued by your city or county)
4. **Zoning Approval or Certificate of Occupancy** (if you operate from a physical location)
5. **Health Department Clearance** (for infused edibles or consumable products)

Check with your:

- State Department of Revenue
- Department of Agriculture
- Local city or county business office

Failing to obtain the proper permits is one of the most common — and expensive — mistakes new dispensary owners make.

Step 6: Protect Yourself and Your Business

Even with proper registration, your dispensary needs layers of protection. Here are the essentials:

◈ **Business Insurance**

- **General liability**: Covers lawsuits from injuries or accidents.
- **Product liability**: Protects you in case a customer claims your product caused harm.
- **Property insurance**: Covers damage or theft (for physical locations).
- **Cyber liability**: Covers data breaches for online stores.

◈ Operating Agreement (even for single-member LLCs)

This outlines how your business operates, who owns what, and how disputes are handled. It helps prevent legal issues, especially if you ever bring on partners.

◈ Legal Disclaimers

Use clear disclaimers in your:

- Product descriptions
- Website footer
- Shipping and return policies
- Marketing materials

Example:

"This product is not intended to diagnose, treat, cure, or prevent any disease. Must be 18 or older to purchase. Use only where legal."

◈ Keep Excellent Records

Create a digital or physical folder with:

- LLC paperwork
- EIN letter
- Bank account statements
- All license copies
- Insurance certificates
- Contracts and supplier agreements

Use cloud storage (e.g., Google Drive, Dropbox) for backup.

◈ **Final Checklist**

Before moving forward, make sure you've completed the following:

◈ Chosen a unique, legal business name

◈ Formed your LLC (and received confirmation)

◈ Obtained your EIN

◈ Opened a business bank account

◈ Registered for any required licenses or permits

◈ Set up insurance and legal disclaimers

◈ Organized all business records in one secure location

Key Takeaways from Chapter 4

- Your business must be **legally structured** to protect your income and personal assets
- An **LLC + EIN + business bank account** forms the foundation of your business identity
- **Licensing and registration** requirements vary by location — don't skip this step
- Legal protections like **insurance, operating agreements, and disclaimers** guard you against risk
- A properly registered business earns **more trust**, qualifies for **funding**, and can **scale confidently**

Chapter 5: Sourcing Legal, High-Quality, Compliant Hemp-Based Products

Now that your dispensary is legally registered and structured, it's time to focus on the **lifeblood of your business**: the products you offer.

Your product line is more than just inventory. It is your reputation, your revenue engine, and the reason customers will come back (or never return). In an industry still battling stigma, misinformation, and inconsistent quality, the businesses that win are the ones who sell **clean, legal, effective, and transparent** hemp products.

In this chapter, you'll learn how to:

- Understand different types of hemp-based products
- Vet suppliers and manufacturers
- Interpret and require proper COAs (Certificates of Analysis)
- Ensure compliance with federal and state regulations
- Choose products that align with your dispensary's brand and mission
- Avoid risky or banned product categories
- Price and profit from your inventory sustainably

Let's build a product line your customers can trust — and one that can scale legally and profitably.

Types of Hemp-Based Products You Can Sell

Under the 2018 Farm Bill, you are legally allowed to sell **hemp-derived products** that contain **less than 0.3% THC by dry weight —** provided they are sourced properly and meet all safety and labeling standards.

Here are the most common categories:

◈ **1. CBD Oils and Tinctures**

- Most recognized and versatile form
- Used for anxiety, pain, sleep, and overall wellness
- Available in full-spectrum, broad-spectrum, or isolate formulas
- Comes in droppers, sprays, and flavored versions

◈ **2. Edibles and Gummies**

- Highly popular and beginner-friendly
- Must clearly label serving size and cannabinoid content
- Should never make medical claims
- Must be compliant with state laws on ingestible hemp

◈ **3. Hemp Flower (Smokable)**

- Looks and smells like marijuana but is legally under 0.3% THC
- Popular with those looking for the ritual of smoking without intoxication
- Banned in some states due to its visual similarity to illegal marijuana

◈ 4. Delta-8 and Other Minor Cannabinoids

- Derived from hemp, offering mild psychoactive effects
- Legal gray area — many states have banned or restricted these
- Must be verified as hemp-derived and tested for purity and potency
- Include clear disclaimers and state-specific shipping restrictions

◈ 5. Topicals (Balms, Creams, Lotions)

- Applied directly to the skin for pain relief or skincare
- Non-psychoactive and generally more widely accepted
- Ideal entry-point products for wellness audiences

◈ 6. Functional Beverages and Infused Foods

- Includes CBD-infused teas, coffees, sparkling water, honey, or protein powders
- Growing niche, but strict rules apply regarding food safety and labeling
- Often require additional food safety licensing in some jurisdictions

◈ 7. Capsules and Softgels

- Pre-measured doses for consumers who dislike oils or edibles
- Offer consistency and discretion
- Must be packaged according to supplement regulations

Certificates of Analysis (COAs): Non-Negotiable

A **Certificate of Analysis (COA)** is a **third-party lab test** that verifies a product's cannabinoid content, purity, and safety. Selling a product without a COA is not only irresponsible — it could lead to legal consequences, customer harm, and the collapse of your brand.

◈ **Your Products MUST Include:**

- **Cannabinoid profile:** Verifies THC content is below 0.3%
- **Contaminant screening:** Checks for pesticides, heavy metals, mold, solvents
- **Batch numbers:** Matches the specific product lot
- **Testing lab contact:** Must be a **verified independent laboratory**, not in-house

◈ **Display COAs on:**

- Your website (downloadable or linked on each product page)
- QR codes on product packaging (where required)
- Printed documents in-store (for physical dispensaries)

If a supplier refuses to provide a COA, walk away — immediately.

How to Vet a Supplier (Your Due Diligence Checklist)

Not all hemp suppliers are created equal. Many businesses in this space cut corners or sell low-quality, improperly sourced, or mislabeled products.

Here's how to **vet a supplier like a pro**:

◈ 1. Source of Hemp

- Hemp must be **grown in the United States**, ideally in regulated states like Colorado, Oregon, Kentucky, or Vermont
- Domestic hemp is more tightly controlled than international sources

◈ 2. Lab Testing Practices

- COAs must be **batch-specific** and from a **third-party ISO-accredited lab**
- Review results for heavy metals, residual solvents, microbial testing, and cannabinoid content

◈ 3. Packaging and Labeling Compliance

- Labels must include:
    - Cannabinoid content per serving
    - Total cannabinoid content per package
    - Ingredients
    - Disclaimers (e.g., "Not evaluated by the FDA")
    - QR code to COA (required in many states)

◈ 4. Licensing and Certifications

- Supplier should be registered with the **state department of agriculture**
- Prefer GMP (Good Manufacturing Practices) or USDA Organic certifications

◈ 5. Customer Service and Communication

- How quickly do they respond?
- Do they offer wholesale rates, white-labeling, or private-label services?
- Are they willing to send samples before your first purchase?

◈ 6. Reputation and Reviews

- Check industry forums, dispensary groups, and business directories
- A single bad review isn't a red flag — but **patterns of complaints are**

Compliant Sourcing Models

◈ 1. Wholesale Distribution

- Buy large quantities at bulk rates
- Store and ship inventory yourself
- Highest profit margins but requires upfront capital and storage space

◈ 2. Affiliate or Drop-Ship Partnerships

- Promote vetted products and earn commission
- Or have orders fulfilled directly from your supplier
- Low startup cost, lower margins, less control

◈ 3. White-Label or Private Label

- Supplier makes the product, you provide your **own branding**
- Requires moderate investment, but builds your **brand equity**
- Ensure COAs still match your branded batch

Products to Avoid (or Handle with Caution)

Some products may **seem profitable** but carry high legal, reputational, or safety risk. Avoid the following unless you fully understand and mitigate the issues:

◈ **High-THC Products (>0.3%)**

- Illegal under federal law unless you're in a licensed marijuana market
- Can result in seizures, fines, or criminal charges

◈ **Unverified Delta-8, Delta-10, HHC**

- Legal in some states, banned in others
- Heavily scrutinized due to chemical synthesis from CBD isolate
- Always check state laws before selling or shipping

◈ **Imported Hemp Extracts**

- Lower safety standards, often contaminated
- May violate labeling and customs requirements

◈ **Any Product with Medical Claims**

- Do not market products as treatments, cures, or therapies
- This invites FDA warning letters and platform bans

Pricing, Profit Margins, and Inventory Management

◈ **Typical Margins:**

- Retail markup for CBD products is typically **100%–300%**
- Topicals and gummies tend to have higher margins
- Wholesale tinctures (cost $8–$15) can retail for $30–$60+

◈ **Inventory Strategy:**

- Start small and scale based on demand
- Use **sample bundles** or **trial kits** to increase average order size
- Monitor expiration dates — hemp products degrade over time

◈ **Track:**

- Cost per unit
- Shipping and packaging costs
- Customer reorder frequency
- Most-viewed product pages (if online)

Your Competitive Edge: Transparency and Trust

The hemp industry is still battling years of misinformation. Many customers are trying these products for the first time. That means your **credibility is your currency**.

Here's how to lead with trust:

- Display lab results clearly
- Answer legal and safety questions in product FAQs
- Avoid hype or exaggerated language
- Build a brand that feels grounded, wellness-oriented, and professional

Key Takeaways from Chapter 5

- Only sell hemp-derived products that contain **under 0.3% THC**
- Every product must include a **valid Certificate of Analysis (COA)** from a **third-party lab**
- Vet your suppliers thoroughly — source only from **domestic, transparent, and compliant manufacturers**
- Avoid products or cannabinoids that are banned or controversial in your shipping areas
- Start with a **small, targeted product line** and grow based on demand
- Your brand reputation depends on **quality, legality, and clarity**

Chapter 6: Smart Marketing in a Restricted Industry

So, your dispensary is registered. Your products are sourced. Your store—whether online or physical—is ready to go.

Now comes the part that **most people get wrong**: marketing.

Promoting a legal hemp dispensary is unlike any other business. You're navigating a tightrope where one wrong word can trigger a shadowban, account removal, or legal issue—even if you're 100% compliant.

In this chapter, we'll dive into:

- Why marketing hemp-based products is uniquely challenging
- The dos and don'ts of compliant advertising
- Powerful organic strategies that work without paid ads
- How to leverage content, education, and SEO
- Building customer trust in a market plagued by skepticism
- Old-school methods that still drive results
- Tools you can use to manage marketing efficiently

Let's build a smart marketing system that keeps your dispensary legal, visible, and growing—without risking everything you've built.

Why Marketing Hemp Is So Complicated

Even though hemp is federally legal, major platforms like **Facebook, Instagram, Google, TikTok, and YouTube** still treat it like contraband. Their advertising policies are often based on **federal laws about marijuana**, or are shaped by **platform liability fears**, not actual legality.

This leads to:

- Rejected ad campaigns
- Suspended business accounts
- Posts getting shadowbanned or hidden
- Limited access to major payment processors

Here's the rule of thumb: **don't rely on paid ads. Build your brand with content, SEO, and direct customer relationships.**

Avoid These Marketing Mistakes (They'll Get You Banned)

◇ **Don't use words like:**

- "Marijuana," "weed," "pot," "stoned," "high"
- "Cures," "treats," "heals," "replaces medication"
- "Guaranteed results," "medical breakthrough"

◇ **Don't post images or videos of:**

- People smoking or vaping
- Large cannabis buds or joints
- Minors or pets near products
- Misleading product comparisons (e.g., showing prescription bottles)

◇ **Don't run Facebook or Google ads unless:**

- You are FDA-approved (which most hemp brands are not)
- You have a verified cannabis license (which won't apply for hemp)
- You have a legal team ready to appeal constantly

Instead, focus your efforts where **you control the channel**.

Compliant Channels That Actually Work

◈ 1. Email Marketing

- One of the **most effective tools** for hemp businesses
- No censorship, direct access to your audience
- Can promote sales, launches, education, and testimonials
- Use free tools to start (Mailerlite, Beehiiv, ConvertKit)

◈ Tips:

- Build your list with opt-ins like "Free CBD eBook" or "10% off your first order"
- Include disclaimers in the footer ("Products not evaluated by the FDA...")
- Send 1–2 times per week with helpful content and updates

◈ 2. Search Engine Optimization (SEO) & Blogging

- Search traffic is evergreen and powerful
- Write blog posts targeting questions your ideal customers search for

◈ Sample blog titles:

- "Is Delta-8 Legal in Texas?"
- "How to Use CBD Oil for Stress Relief"
- "Best CBD Products for Beginners"
- "CBD vs. THC: What's the Difference?"
- "Can I Travel with CBD?"

◈ Add keywords, images, disclaimers, and links to products
◈ Post to your blog, Medium, and LinkedIn for extra reach

◈ 3. Educational Content on YouTube or Podcasts

- YouTube Shorts and podcast interviews are under-moderated compared to Meta
- Focus on **education, not direct selling**

◈ Talk about:

- The science behind cannabinoids
- Your startup journey and why you started
- How to read a COA
- What to look for in safe hemp products
- Hemp myths debunked

◈ Use subtitles, brand visuals, and always add disclaimers

◈ 4. QR Codes and Print Marketing

Old-school tools that work **extremely well in restricted industries**:

- Add QR codes to:
  - Business cards
  - Flyers
  - Product packaging
  - Stickers
  - Table tents at pop-ups
  - Event posters
- QR links should lead to:
  - A mobile-friendly product page
  - An email signup form
  - A custom funnel (via platforms like Involve.me)

◈ Tip: Design print materials in Canva or Adobe Express for a professional look

◈ **5. Organic Social Media (Play It Smart)**

Platforms like Instagram, TikTok, and Threads **can still work**—just don't treat them like sales machines.

◈ Focus on:

- Educational content
- Lifestyle reels
- Behind-the-scenes footage
- Day-in-the-life posts
- Customer testimonials
- Fun, trending content (without product use)

Avoid showing:

- Smoke, vapes, or packaging that looks like marijuana
- Medical-style claims or anything targeting illness
- Pricing or "limited time" discount offers

◈ Think of social media as a **brand awareness engine**, not a direct selling tool.

Build Trust with Transparency

In a space full of confusion, **transparency is your marketing superpower.** Customers are skeptical, and rightly so. Your job is to earn trust with:

◇ **What to Share Publicly:**

- COAs for every product (easy to find, clear QR codes)
- Real customer reviews (with permission)
- Shipping policies, refund terms, and disclaimers
- Content that explains how your products are made and tested
- A professional, secure-looking website

◇ The more transparent you are, the more likely people will try your products over competitors who hide behind vague claims or questionable sourcing.

Events, Pop-Ups, and Local Partnerships

Don't underestimate **offline marketing**. Hemp-based businesses thrive at events and in-person gatherings:

◈ **Try:**

- Farmer's markets
- Holistic expos
- Yoga studios
- Wellness retreats
- Boutique partnerships
- Community college campuses (18+ only)

Bring:

- Free samples
- Educational flyers
- QR codes to shop
- Email sign-up incentives
- Dispensary-branded merchandise

In-person trust converts into long-term online sales.

Customer Loyalty & Referral Programs

Once you have a few customers, make them your **ambassadors**:

◇ **Offer**:

- Referral discounts ("Give 10%, Get 10%")
- Loyalty rewards (points for every dollar spent)
- VIP early access to new drops
- Subscriber-only coupons or bundles

◇ **Bundle example:**

- "Calm Starter Kit" with oil + gummies + balm
- "Delta Discovery Kit" (only if legal in your area)
- "Hemp Travel Pack" for on-the-go relief

Keep it fun, repeatable, and full of value.

Tools to Power Your Marketing

Here are recommended tools to streamline your work:

Category	Tool	Purpose
Email Marketing	Beehiiv, Mailerlite	Build and automate email list
Design & Branding	Canva	Create flyers, IG posts, QR cards
Funnel Creation	Involve.me	Create lead quizzes, sign-ups
Blogging & SEO	Medium, Word-Press	Build search traffic organically
Analytics	Google Analytics	Track website performance
Scheduling	Later, Buffer	Pre-plan social media content
Review Collection	Loox, Judge.me	Gather and display customer reviews

Key Takeaways from Chapter 6

- Don't rely on paid ads — build a marketing strategy focused on **content, education, and community**
- Avoid banned keywords, images, and claims that trigger platform shutdowns
- Leverage **email**, **SEO blogging**, and **offline tools** like flyers and QR codes
- Transparency builds **credibility**, which drives customer conversion and loyalty
- Focus on long-term growth, not short-term hype — this is how you build a **lasting dispensary brand**

Chapter 7: Financial Survival — Funding, Cash Flow, and Banking in the Hemp Space

You've built the legal foundation. You've sourced compliant, quality products. You've even started building attention through smart marketing.

But here's the truth: **attention is not income** — and visibility means nothing if your business isn't financially stable.

The harsh reality is that hemp-based businesses face unique challenges:

- Traditional banks may refuse service
- Payment processors can suddenly shut you down
- You may have difficulty getting loans or business credit
- Many funding programs exclude hemp-based businesses entirely

So how do you build a **financially resilient dispensary** in a system that wasn't designed to support you?

This chapter answers that — in detail.

We'll cover:

- Opening the right financial accounts
- Managing cash flow and reinvestment
- Finding funding sources despite banking discrimination
- Creating a lean budget and profit-first mindset
- Protecting income from taxes, penalties, and risk
- Preparing your dispensary for scale or exit

This isn't just about surviving. It's about thriving.

Why Money Is Treated Differently in This Industry

Even though hemp is federally legal (as long as it contains <0.3% THC), the financial system still lumps your business into a "high-risk" category — the same category used for gambling, adult entertainment, and firearms.

This leads to:

- Rejected business bank applications
- Sudden shutdown of Stripe, PayPal, or Square accounts
- No access to traditional business loans
- Increased fees and slower transaction approvals
- Insurance requirements just to open accounts

This isn't paranoia. It's reality — and you must prepare for it.

Step 1: Open the Right Business Bank Account
You **must** keep your personal and business finances separate.
But not every bank is willing to work with you.

◈ **Look For:**

- Local banks and credit unions with cannabis/hemp experience
- Fintech companies that specialize in high-risk industries
- Business checking accounts with low monthly fees and flexible limits

◈ **Required documents:**

- LLC formation docs
- EIN from the IRS
- Business address
- Business description (be honest but use non-inflammatory terms like "wellness," "herbal," "natural supplements")

◈ Pro Tip: Avoid terms like "CBD store" or "cannabis shop" in your initial application unless you know the bank allows them.

Step 2: Use Safe Payment Processors (Avoid Getting Shut Down)

The biggest mistake new dispensary owners make is using **Stripe, PayPal, or Venmo** for transactions.

These platforms **prohibit** hemp and CBD sales—even if you're compliant. They'll freeze your funds with no warning.

◈ **Approved Payment Processors for Hemp Businesses:**

- Square (CBD program — must apply separately)
- Authorize.Net (with a high-risk merchant account)
- NMI + merchant partners
- DigiPay, PayKings, Easy Pay Direct (specialize in high-risk)

You'll often pay **2.9%–6% per transaction**, which is higher than typical businesses. Build this into your pricing model.

◈ Always get a written confirmation that your product type is allowed.

Step 3: Budget Like a Lean Startup

Every dollar matters. Most hemp startups fail due to poor financial planning — not because they lacked passion or customers.

Create a **30/30/30/10 model**:

- 30%: Product restock
- 30%: Marketing, email, branding
- 30%: Operating costs (rent, supplies, insurance)
- 10%: Emergency reserves or reinvestment cushion

Track every cent using tools like:

- Wave (free accounting)
- QuickBooks (paid, industry standard)
- Google Sheets (manual, flexible)

◈ Do a **weekly money check-in**:

- What came in?
- What went out?
- Where are you overspending?
- What's your reorder point for inventory?

Step 4: Where to Find Funding (Even When Banks Say No)

You may not qualify for SBA loans or traditional business credit — but funding still exists.

⬦ **Funding Options for Hemp Businesses:**

1. Personal Investment (Bootstrapping)

- Use your savings carefully
- Maintain a tight burn rate
- Best control, but limited scale

2. Crowdfunding

- Platforms like FundRazr and StartEngine allow CBD/hemp campaigns
- Focus on your story, transparency, and impact
- Offer perks, samples, or behind-the-scenes access

3. Private Investors / Angel Networks

- Find cannabis-specific angel investor groups
- Have your COAs, business plan, and margins ready
- Be prepared for negotiation and equity offers

4. Community Development Financial Institutions (CDFIs)

- Local lenders that may support underserved entrepreneurs
- Less judgmental about industry type
- Often offer mentorship along with funding

5. Grants for Entrepreneurs

- Focus on business development programs for women, minorities, or rural startups
- Not always cannabis-specific, but you can position your brand as wellness-focused
- Search for state-based small business grant directories

◈ Avoid predatory lenders or companies offering **"fast hemp loans"** with 30%+ interest rates.

Step 5: Protecting Your Income from Taxes and Fines

Because this industry is under intense scrutiny, **you must document everything**.

◈ **Keep:**

- Receipts
- COAs
- Contracts with suppliers
- Proof of insurance
- Monthly inventory logs

Work with a tax professional who:

- Understands Schedule C or S-corp filings
- Has hemp/CBD client experience
- Helps you track write-offs legally (advertising, software, inventory loss, office space, mileage)

◈ Some states tax hemp products **differently** than other supplements. Know your local laws.

Step 6: Build a Profit-First System
Instead of waiting until year-end to "see what's left," flip the script.

◇ **Profit-First Formula:**

1. Income comes in
2. You immediately take a small fixed **profit slice** (even 5%)
3. Allocate the rest across expenses, product costs, etc.
4. Reinvest the profit into scaling or saving

◇ **Use separate accounts:**

- Income
- Profit
- Operating expenses
- Tax reserve
- Inventory

When you operate this way, your dispensary becomes sustainable—even when growth is slow.

Step 7: Prepare for Long-Term Financial Success

Think ahead. What if you want to:

- Sell the business?
- Franchise it?
- Get acquired?
- License your product line?

You'll need:

- Clean bookkeeping
- Documented growth trends
- Verified supply chain
- Brand equity (e.g., domain ownership, product IP, customer list)

◈ A healthy business isn't just profitable — it's **valuable**.
Even if you never sell, you want a dispensary that creates **wealth, not just income.**

Key Takeaways from Chapter 7

- Separate your business finances with compliant banks and processors
- Use financial tools and weekly check-ins to track everything
- Create a lean budget and protect every dollar
- Don't wait for banks — explore funding from investors, grants, and CDFIs
- Work with a tax pro to stay legal and avoid penalties
- Prioritize profit, not just revenue
- Prepare now for the possibility of exit, sale, or expansion

Chapter 8: Building a Loyal Customer Base — Experience, Education, and Trust

At this point, you've done the hard work most dispensary founders never complete.

- You've structured your business legally.
- You've sourced compliant, high-quality products.
- You've crafted a smart marketing strategy.
- You've built a financial framework that protects your growth.

But there's one final piece — and it's the one that separates long-term success from burnout:
Creating a customer experience that turns one-time buyers into lifelong believers.

In the hemp and wellness space, **trust is your most valuable asset**. You are not just selling a product. You are helping people change their routine, regulate their emotions, and shift their health narrative. That requires care, education, and consistency.

This chapter explores how to:

- Deliver exceptional customer service, both online and in-person
- Build educational systems that empower your buyers
- Address common fears and misconceptions about hemp products
- Encourage referrals and community engagement
- Scale trust through transparency, follow-up, and story
- Turn customers into advocates, not just consumers

Because at the end of the day, a customer who **believes in your mission** will spend more, return often, and promote your dispensary better than any ad ever could.

1. First Impressions: The Dispensary Experience

Whether your store is digital or physical, your **presentation is everything**.

People are still cautious around hemp, CBD, and minor cannabinoids. Their first visit must calm their fears and boost their confidence.

For Online Stores:

◈ Clean, modern layout

◈ Clear categories: oils, gummies, topicals, etc.

◈ Product photos with high resolution

◈ Labels that match COAs

◈ Easy-to-read descriptions (no hype or medical claims)

◈ FAQ page with legal and safety info

◈ SSL-secured checkout with clear payment options

◈ Tip: Use **trust-building visuals** like:

- Third-party lab badges
- "Veteran-owned," "Black-owned," or "Family business" labels
- Photos of your founder or packaging process
- Verified customer reviews

For Physical Stores:

◈ Friendly, informed staff

◈ Samples and testers (where legal)

◈ Organized layout and good lighting

◈ Clear educational signage

◈ Flyers, business cards, or QR codes to your website

◈ Music and scent that matches your brand mood (calming, energizing, etc.)

First impressions should answer this silent question every customer has:

"Is this a legitimate, safe, and thoughtful place?"

2. Addressing Fear and Misconceptions

Most new customers are scared of one of three things:

- Getting high unintentionally
- Breaking the law
- Wasting money on a "scam" product

You must address all three through **reassurance and education.**

◈ **Key Info to Include in Every Interaction:**

- "This product contains less than 0.3% THC and is federally legal."
- "Here's the COA that shows exactly what's inside."
- "We don't use fillers or artificial ingredients."
- "Every product is tested for safety, purity, and cannabinoid content."

◈ Proactive trust-building phrases:

- "Start with half a gummy if you're new to cannabinoids."
- "You will not feel intoxicated — but you may feel more relaxed."
- "You can legally ship this anywhere in [your state or country]."
- "This product isn't about getting high — it's about getting balanced."

Trust doesn't just come from accuracy. It comes from **compassion.**

3. Educating Your Customers Like They're Family

Education is your **highest-converting marketing tool.** The more your customers understand hemp, the more they buy.

Educational Tools That Sell:

- Beginner's guide eBook ("How to Use CBD with Confidence")
- Printed pamphlets with usage tips and dosage notes
- YouTube videos walking through your product line
- Weekly blog posts answering common questions
- Live Q&A sessions on Instagram or Threads
- FAQ cards with every order

You can create these once and reuse them forever.

◈ Consider packing each order with:

- A welcome note
- A how-to-use guide
- A QR code to join your email list
- A coupon for their next order
- A card asking for honest reviews or feedback

4. Turning Buyers into Believers

After the first sale, your job isn't over. That's when it **really begins.** The goal is to **guide** the customer through an experience that feels intentional and personal.

The 3-Step Retention Sequence:

◈ Step 1: The Follow-Up

Send an email or text:

- "Your order has shipped."
- "Your order arrived—need help getting started?"
- "Here's how to get the most out of your new product."

◈ Step 2: The Check-In

After 7–10 days:

- "How are you feeling?"
- "Are you noticing any effects?"
- "Need help adjusting your dose?"

◈ Step 3: The Invite

After 2–3 weeks:

- "Leave a review and get a discount."
- "Join our community page or referral program."
- "Here's what we recommend next based on your first order."

This level of **engagement creates emotional loyalty**, not just transactional loyalty.

5. Creating a Community Around Your Brand

Your customers want to feel like part of something **bigger** than just buying a product.

Create a community around:

- Wellness and empowerment
- Plant-based education
- Natural recovery stories
- Mental clarity and calm
- Fighting stigma around alternative medicine

You can do this with:

- A private Facebook or Discord group
- Regular newsletters
- Hashtag campaigns (e.g., #MyCBDStory)
- Customer spotlight posts
- Live classes or interviews with herbalists, athletes, or therapists

◈ Tip: Feature your customers and their stories (with permission). They are your best ambassadors.

6. Scaling Trust Without Losing Your Soul

As you grow, the biggest threat isn't competition — it's losing your personal touch.

To keep scaling without becoming robotic:

- Keep answering customer questions in your own voice
- Use automation to **enhance**, not replace, connection
- Rotate personal stories or updates into emails
- Send free gifts or bonus products to loyal customers
- Show up online with consistency — not perfection

◇ Remember: A customer doesn't just remember what they bought.
They remember how you **made them feel.**

Key Takeaways from Chapter 8

- First impressions — whether online or in-person — shape everything
- Address fears around legality, safety, and effectiveness with clear communication
- Use education as a long-term selling tool: blogs, videos, guides, and FAQs
- Follow up with buyers to build emotional trust and repeat business
- Build a community that sees your dispensary as more than a store — it's a lifestyle
- Don't lose your soul as you scale — human connection is your strongest asset

Final Words: From Legal Paperwork to Lifelong Impact

What began as a business idea is now a living brand — one with the power to transform lives.

By choosing to do this the legal, ethical, and transparent way, you are helping reshape the hemp industry for the better. You are empowering customers to take charge of their wellness. You are proving that small businesses, even in restricted spaces, can thrive without cutting corners.

This isn't just about selling gummies or oils.

It's about creating a **movement of trust**, health, and holistic business.

The journey doesn't end here.

Let your dispensary be a place of education, honesty, and light — where legality and humanity walk hand in hand.

You're not just in business.

You're in service.

And now, you're ready.

Conclusion: From Startup to Legacy

You've arrived at the final page of this guide, but this is just the beginning of your journey.

By now, you've equipped yourself with the knowledge to do what very few dare to do — **legally launch, build, and scale a dispensary business** in one of the most scrutinized, misunderstood, and opportunity-rich industries of our time.

You've learned how to:

- Structure your business entity and register it properly
- Choose between physical and online dispensary models
- Source safe, legal, compliant hemp-based products
- Navigate high-risk payment processors and financial systems
- Market your dispensary without triggering bans or shutdowns
- Build lasting trust through education and exceptional service
- Reinforce financial stability while planning for long-term growth

These are not small accomplishments. These are the foundational steps of a **legacy business**—not a trend, not a hustle, but something enduring, reputable, and deeply rooted in purpose.

But knowledge alone isn't enough.

The difference between a side hustle and a legacy brand is execution.

It's in your daily actions:

- Filing that paperwork instead of putting it off
- Making that follow-up call to a vendor or customer
- Publishing your first blog post, even if it's not perfect
- Showing up again tomorrow, and the day after that
- Choosing ethics and transparency over shortcuts and noise

Every empire begins with a small, intentional decision. And now, you've got the blueprint to make the right ones.

You are not just building a business — you are becoming a **steward of trust** in an industry that desperately needs honest, dependable voices.

You are not just selling products — you are giving people tools for wellness, peace, and empowerment.

You are not just another startup — you are part of the **green gold rush**, a once-in-a-generation opportunity to build something real, lawful, and powerful.

You are no longer on the sidelines.

You are in the game — as a founder, a creator, a leader.

Whether your dispensary stays local or grows into a multi-state powerhouse... whether you sell 10 products or 10,000... whether your story is just beginning or already unfolding...

You have everything you need to create more than a business.

You have what it takes to create a legacy.

Now take action.

Begin legally.

Grow ethically.

And never stop building.

Because the future of this industry — and your place in it — is not written in lawbooks or licensing offices.

It's written by those bold enough to build it.

Appendix A: Suggested Tools

Here's what you might use for your dispensary journey.

Launching and operating a legal, compliant, and sustainable dispensary doesn't require an expensive tech stack — but it **does** require smart, efficient tools that help you operate like a true business from Day One.

Below is a categorized breakdown of **recommended tools** for business setup, sourcing, marketing, finances, and ongoing education. These suggestions are tool *types* and categories, not endorsements of specific brands.

These tools can help you operate lean, move faster, and remain legally sound while scaling your dispensary over time.

1. Business Setup Tools

Before you begin selling any product, these tools will help you **form a legal structure**, file required documentation, and protect yourself as a business entity.

◈ LLC Formation Services:

- Use services that offer simplified filing, name checks, operating agreement templates, and compliance alerts.
- Choose an option that offers state-specific guidance for cannabis and hemp-related businesses.
- Consider services that include annual reporting and registered agent representation.

◈ IRS EIN Registration:

- Apply directly through the IRS portal to obtain your Employer Identification Number (EIN).
- This is essential for setting up a business bank account, filing taxes, and hiring if needed.
- EINs are free to register — never pay for this unless bundled into a full setup package.

◈ Business Legal Services:

- Look for platforms that provide contract templates, legal consulting, or access to cannabis-aware attorneys.
- Ideal services include NDAs, partnership agreements, product liability disclaimers, and website policies.
- Some may also assist with intellectual property protection, like trademarks and branding.

2. Product Sources

The core of your dispensary is the product — it must be safe, tested, and compliant.

◈ Verified Hemp Suppliers with COAs:

- Choose vendors that provide a **Certificate of Analysis (COA)** for every product and batch.
- Ensure they use **third-party testing labs** and comply with the 2018 Farm Bill (<0.3% THC).
- Look for transparent ingredient sourcing, sustainable farming practices, and good turnaround times.

◈ Affiliate or Wholesale Product Vendors:

- If you're not manufacturing, work with white-label or private-label hemp manufacturers.
- Consider affiliate platforms with legal product lines and compliance standards.
- Many suppliers offer tiered pricing, MOQ (minimum order quantity) discounts, and branded packaging options.

3. Marketing Tools

Marketing in the hemp space requires subtlety, strategy, and smart tools. These help you **educate, promote, and stay visible**—without breaking platform policies.

◈ Email Newsletter Builders:

- Choose tools that allow automated drip sequences, landing pages, and segmentation.
- Must support high-risk industries or provide approval paths for hemp-related content.
- Look for drag-and-drop editors, mobile optimization, and integration with your shop platform.

◈ QR Code Generators:

- Use to link to educational blog posts, product pages, or email sign-up funnels.
- Choose options that allow customization (logo, color, frame) and analytics tracking.
- Ideal for business cards, packaging, in-store posters, or event handouts.

◈ Graphic Design Tools (Logos, Flyers):

- Use design platforms with templates for social media, postcards, product labels, and pitch decks.
- Look for platforms that allow brand kits, resizing tools, and transparent backgrounds.
- Good tools help you appear professional even without a design background.

◈ **Blog and SEO Tools:**

- Content management systems and keyword research tools help your blog rank in search engines.
- Use writing platforms that suggest headlines, subheadings, and keyword density.
- Also consider scheduling tools for sharing blog content across social platforms automatically.

4. Accounting & Bookkeeping Tools

The financial health of your dispensary relies on **precise tracking, smart budgeting, and tax readiness.**

◈ **Free Bookkeeping Tools:**

- Ideal for startups with limited income who need to track expenses manually.
- Often include invoice templates, receipt uploads, profit/loss dashboards, and basic reporting.
- Some tools connect directly to your bank account for automatic categorization.

◈ **Paid Options for Business Finances:**

- More robust tools include automated payroll, tax estimation, vendor payments, and inventory tracking.
- Look for platforms that support multiple users (e.g., accountant access), cloud backups, and integration with ecommerce.
- Hemp businesses may need support for high-risk merchant accounts — ask customer service before committing.

5. Learning & Industry Resources

Staying ahead means **learning continuously** — especially in a rapidly evolving legal landscape. These resources can help you stay informed and inspired.

◈ Hemp Industry News Sites:

- Look for independent, journalist-run platforms reporting on hemp legislation, industry trends, and business analysis.
- Use these to stay up to date on state laws, FDA regulations, new cannabinoid research, and supplier recalls.

◈ Podcasts for Cannabis and Wellness Business:

- Listen to interviews with founders, scientists, marketers, and legal professionals.
- Learn how other dispensaries grew their brands, avoided pitfalls, and developed niche audiences.
- Podcast episodes often cover marketing strategies, legal updates, or funding advice specific to hemp.

◈ YouTube for SEO and Growth Tutorials:

- Search for small business creators sharing tutorials on:
    - Starting an online store
    - Optimizing Google search visibility
    - Building email funnels
    - Hemp legality breakdowns by state
- Watch interviews with top CBD brand founders and listen to how they scaled.

Final Thoughts on Tools

The **right tools don't run your business** — but they let you run it more smoothly, legally, and efficiently. Choose what works for your current scale, revisit what you use every quarter, and don't be afraid to switch tools as your dispensary grows.

Start lean. Stay smart.

And always make room for learning — because in the hemp space, **adaptation is survival**.

Appendix B: Sample Budget — Lean Model for Online Start

Launching an online dispensary doesn't require six figures — but it does require **intentional, efficient spending**. This appendix outlines a **lean startup budget** designed for those entering the hemp and CBD space with minimal upfront capital.

Whether you're bootstrapping, building after hours, or launching solo, this budget reflects **realistic startup costs** without unnecessary fluff. Every line item is designed to get you live, legal, and selling — without taking on debt or risking regulatory violations.

Below is a detailed estimate of each startup expense for an **online-only model**, assuming you're either selling third-party hemp products or drop-shipping from a legal supplier.

Lean Dispensary Startup Budget Breakdown

Item	Estimated Cost	Details
LLC Formation	$49–$199 (+ state fees)	Use an affordable LLC filing service or file yourself through your Secretary of State. State fees vary from $40 to $500 depending on jurisdiction.
EIN	Free	Apply directly through the IRS website. Do not pay for this unless bundled with other services.

Item	Estimated Cost	Details
Domain Name	$12–$20/year	Choose a clean, brandable domain (.com preferred) for your dispensary or wellness brand.
Logo Design	$0–$50	Use free design tools or hire a beginner freelancer. Quality logos can be obtained affordably.
Online Store Setup	$25–$100/month	Includes ecommerce platform subscription, secure checkout, and basic templates. Shopify, Wix, or Square Online are good starting points.
Initial Inventory	$10–$300	Start with a small amount of top sellers (e.g., gummies, tinctures, topicals). This number is scalable based on your supplier type.

Item	Estimated Cost	Details
Shipping	$15–$40	Covers packaging, postage, and any initial mailing supplies. Use flat-rate boxes to keep costs predictable.
Email Platform	Free–$49/month	Start with a free plan that includes automated sequences, opt-in forms, and 500–2,000 subscribers.
Marketing Materials	$30–$75	Includes flyers, stickers, QR code cards, business cards, and digital graphics. Focus on education, branding, and first impressions.

◈ **Total Estimated Range: $175–$800**

This budget allows you to:

- Operate legally
- Own your brand
- Start testing your market
- Begin gathering testimonials
- Ship product immediately
- Begin building a loyal customer base

Optional add-ons (not included in the budget above):

- Business insurance (strongly recommended once sales grow)
- Paid ads (only after organic methods are in place)
- Professional photos or product packaging
- Paid legal consultations or copywriting services

◈ **Lean Launch Checklist**

This is your action-oriented roadmap for launch. Once each section is complete, you're legally positioned to begin sales and growth.

Business Setup

- ◈ Choose a legal and brand-safe business name
- ◈ Register your LLC through your state or a filing service
- ◈ Apply for a free EIN from the IRS
- ◈ Open a business checking account at a compliant bank
- ◈ Obtain state or local licenses (if applicable for hemp resale or operation)

Online Store Setup

- ◈ Choose an ecommerce platform (Shopify, Square, etc.)
- ◈ Upload each product with detailed description, disclaimers, and COAs (Certificates of Analysis)
- ◈ Connect your custom domain
- ◈ Set up secure payment processor (hemp-compliant only)
- ◈ Add shipping zones, rates, and tracking integration
- ◈ Include refund policy, terms of use, and privacy notice

Branding

- ◈ Create or upload your logo and branded images
- ◈ Write a clear brand story or "About" page
- ◈ Add your first 2–3 blog or educational posts (product usage, legality, beginner's guide)
- ◈ Set up a branded QR code funnel (leading to blog, shop, or sign-up)

Marketing

- ◇ Design and print business cards, flyers, or educational hand-outs
- ◇ Set up social media accounts under your brand name
- ◇ Start posting organic content (product info, behind-the-scenes, educational graphics)
- ◇ Encourage first customers to leave testimonials or reviews
- ◇ Collect email addresses from early interest and provide incentives

Operations

- ◇ Set up a basic bookkeeping tool (manual spreadsheet or free software)
- ◇ Log every startup expense and recurring cost
- ◇ Monitor evolving laws (state and federal) monthly
- ◇ Evaluate and rotate product offerings based on feedback and sales
- ◇ Reinvest a percentage of early profits into upgrades, inventory, or outreach

Final Notes

A lean launch is not a limited one — it's **an efficient one**. By prioritizing only what's essential, you reduce startup risk, avoid waste, and allow your brand to evolve with customer feedback.

Use this budget and checklist as a compass — not a cage. As your dispensary grows, your needs will evolve. But if you follow these basics, you'll begin from a place of **clarity, legality, and long-term potential**.

www.ingramcontent.com/pod-product-compliance
Lightning Source LLC
Chambersburg PA
CBHW052112150726
48002CB00006B/2321